EVOLVE

WORKBOOK

Octavio Ramírez Espinosa

2B

Shaftesbury Road, Cambridge CB2 8EA, United Kingdom

One Liberty Plaza, 20th Floor, New York, NY 10006, USA

477 Williamstown Road, Port Melbourne, VIC 3207, Australia

314–321, 3rd Floor, Plot 3, Splendor Forum, Jasola District Centre, New Delhi – 110025, India

103 Penang Road, #05-06/07, Visioncrest Commercial, Singapore 238467

Cambridge University Press & Assessment is a department of the University of Cambridge.

We share the University's mission to contribute to society through the pursuit of education, learning and research at the highest international levels of excellence.

www.cambridge.org
Information on this title: www.cambridge.org/9781108411929

First published 2019

20 19 18 17 16 15 14 13 12 11

Printed in Poland by Opolgraf

A catalogue record for this publication is available from the British Library

ISBN 978-1-108-40524-9 Student's Book
ISBN 978-1-108-40505-8 Student's Book A
ISBN 978-1-108-40917-9 Student's Book B
ISBN 978-1-108-40526-3 Student's Book with Practice Extra
ISBN 978-1-108-40506-5 Student's Book with Practice Extra A
ISBN 978-1-108-40919-3 Student's Book with Practice Extra B
ISBN 978-1-108-40898-1 Workbook with Audio
ISBN 978-1-108-40863-9 Workbook with Audio A
ISBN 978-1-108-41192-9 Workbook with Audio B
ISBN 978-1-108-40516-4 Teacher's Edition with Test Generator
ISBN 978-1-108-41065-6 Presentation Plus
ISBN 978-1-108-41202-5 Class Audio CDs
ISBN 978-1-108-40788-5 Video Resource Book with DVD
ISBN 978-1-108-41446-3 Full Contact with DVD
ISBN 978-1-108-41153-0 Full Contact with DVD A
ISBN 978-1-108-41412-8 Full Contact with DVD B

Additional resources for this publication at www.cambridge.org/evolve

CONTENTS

1 VOCABULARY: Naming food

A **Look at the pictures and complete the crossword.**

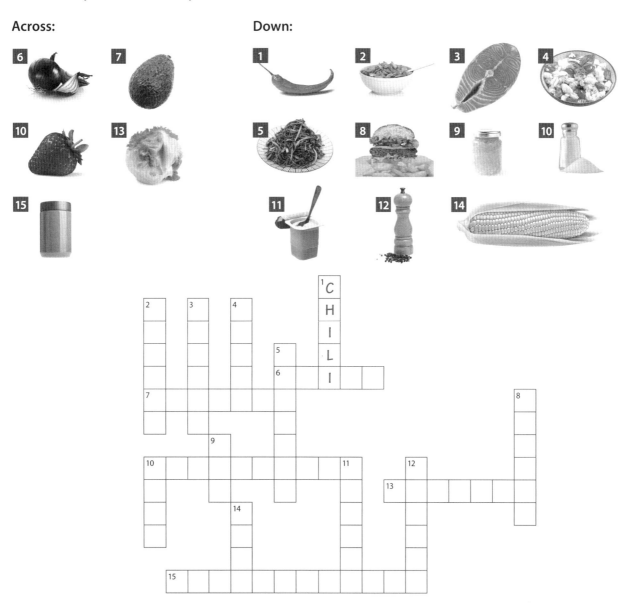

Across:

Down:

2 GRAMMAR: Quantifiers

A Circle the correct words to complete the questions.

1 How *much* / *many* bowls of cereal and how *much* / *many* fruit do you eat every day?

2 How *much* / *many* burgers and how *much* / *many* salmon do you eat each week?

3 How *much* / *many* salt and pepper do you add to your food?

4 How *much* / *many* pasta and how *much* / *many* chilies do you eat in a week?

B **Correct the sentences using the words in the box.**

| a little | a lot | many | much | some |

1 I'm putting many of onion in my salad.
   I'm putting a lot of onion in my salad.

2 You just need a few blueberry jam to add flavor.

   _____

3 I'm adding a few yogurt to my bowl of fruit.

   _____

4 There are too much noodles to put them all in one bowl.

   _____

5 We added too many salt to our dinner.

   _____

6 Let's add a few more pepper to the pasta.

   _____

3 GRAMMAR AND VOCABULARY

A **Complete the conversation below with your own information.**

A Do you remember your favorite comfort food when you were a kid?

B Yes, I do. It was ¹_____.

A And how *much / many* ²_____ did you eat in a week?

B I think I ate *a lot of / some / a few / a little* ³_____ every week.

A What did you like to eat it with?

B I loved to eat it with ⁴_____.

A How *much / many* ⁵_____ do you eat now?

B I eat *a lot / some / a few / a little*.

A What's your favorite comfort food now?

B It's ⁶_____, but I also eat *a lot of / some / a few / a little* ⁷_____ every week.

1 VOCABULARY: Describing food

A **Complete the sentences with the words in the box.**

bitter	~~boiled~~	delicious	fresh	fried
grilled	raw	roasted	sour	spicy

1 I hate _____boiled_____ eggs in my salad!
2 This lemon is too _____ for me.
3 I prefer a _____ salad for lunch.
4 Those chilies are very _____, but I don't mind hot foods.
5 In some Japanese foods, the fish is _____. They don't cook it.
6 I usually don't add sugar to my coffee, but this one is too _____!
7 The meat comes with _____ onions and peppers. Everything is cooked at the same time.
8 Thanks for cooking dinner. It was really _____! Is there more?
9 I planned on making _____ chicken for dinner tomorrow, but my oven is not working.
10 Are you having some _____ potatoes with your burger?

2 GRAMMAR: Verb patterns

A **Put the words in the correct order to make sentences.**

1 for / I / stand / my / waiting / can't / food.
   I can't stand waiting for my food.
2 food truck / the / ordering / love / from / We / on the corner.
   _____
3 than to / cook / prefers to / dinner / Ali / go out.
   _____
4 mind / in / I / waiting / don't / line.
   _____
5 own / cooking / you / like / your / Do / meals?
   _____
6 order / like / the / to / would / He / grilled salmon.
   _____
7 eating / Do / enjoy / you / spicy food?
   _____
8 hate / We / the dishes / doing / after dinner.
   _____
9 want / Do / eat out / they / to / on Friday night?
   _____

B **Circle** the correct words to complete the sentences.

1 My best friend loves _____ Indian food.

    a eat   **b** to eat   **c** ate

2 Claire would like _____ for us tonight.

    a to cook   **b** cooking   **c** cook

3 Do you want _____ dessert as well?

    a ordering   **b** ordered   **c** to order

4 I _____ waiting a few more minutes.

    a don't mind   **b** want   **c** woud like

5 She _____ to add spicy sauce to her Mexican food.

    a enjoys   **b** can't stand   **c** loves

6 I want _____ you out for dinner tomorrow. Are you free?

    a to take   **b** taking   **c** take

3 GRAMMAR AND VOCABULARY

A **Think about a food truck or restaurant you know. Write some opinions for their comments page. Use the words in the box for ideas.**

delicious	eat raw food	fried	have fresh food
have more sauce options	have the same food	order online	~~try new food~~
types of sauce	wait for the check	wait to order	

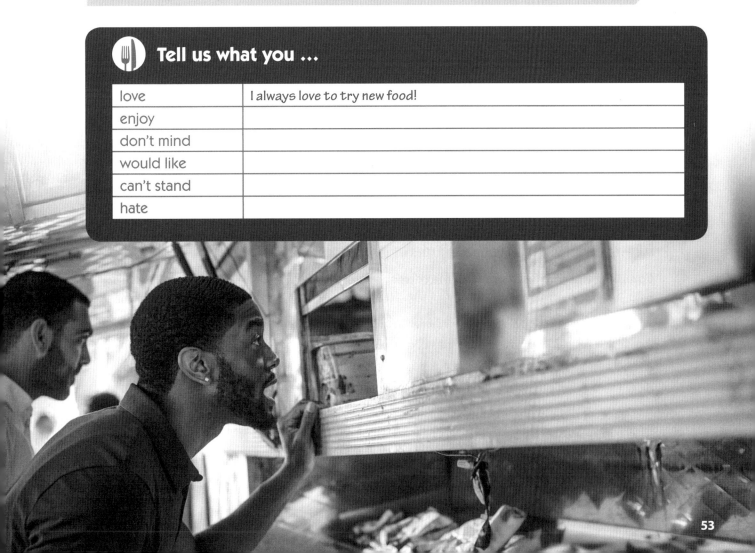

🍴 Tell us what you ...

love	I always love to try new food!
enjoy	
don't mind	
would like	
can't stand	
hate	

I'LL HAVE THE CHICKEN

1 FUNCTIONAL LANGUAGE: Ordering food and taking food orders

A **Put the conversation in order.**

☐ Oh, I'm allergic to nuts.

☐ Perfect! I'll be right back.

☐ It comes with avocado, tomatoes, potatoes, peanuts, and the house dressing.

☐ Well, today's special is the chicken salad.

☐ Oh, OK. No nuts. Anything to drink?

☐ OK, we can add almonds instead.

1 Hi, are you ready to order?

☐ I mean, I'm allergic to <u>all</u> kinds of nuts.

☐ What does it come with?

☐ I'll have a soda.

☐ Yes, what do you recommend?

2 REAL-WORLD STRATEGY: *I mean*

A **Complete the conversations with the correct expressions.**

B Excuse me? What [1] <u>comes with</u> the burger?

A It comes with lettuce, tomato, and avocado.

B [2] _____, do French fries come with it?

A You can have French fries and a drink for two dollars more.

B Oh, OK. [3] _____ just a burger, please.

A How was the food?

B It was very good, thanks.

A [4] _____ some dessert?

B Not today, thanks. [5] _____?

A Sure. Here you go.

54

3 FUNCTIONAL LANGUAGE AND REAL-WORLD STRATEGY

A Read the situations in the chart. Write the correct response to the questions and suggestions.

	Server	You
You are allergic to milk.	"The chef says there is some yogurt in the dressing."	I mean, I can't have any milk at all.
You are on a diet.	"Can I get you a dessert?"	
You are vegetarian.	"The soup is made with chicken, rice, and vegetables."	
You want to order dessert.	"Would you like anything else?"	
You ordered the grilled salmon.	"Here's your order, fried fish with grilled vegetables."	

B Choose one of the situations about diets in exercise A. Think of an idea for a food truck that sells food for people with this special diet. Complete the chart below with the information about your food truck.

The name of your food truck:	
Who your customers are:	
Specials and how they are cooked:	
The price of your food:	

7.4 IMPOSSIBLE FOODS

1 LISTENING

A ◀)) **7.01** **Listen to the radio interviews. Number the speakers in the order you hear them.**

- ☐ Keila Summers, regular customer at The Origins restaurant
- ☐ Melissa Poitras, vegetarian and animal lover
- ☐ Charles Davis, chef at The Origins restaurant
- ☐ Carol Saint Vincent, restaurant writer

The Origins restaurant invites you to a special event

Be the first to try our **MEAT-FREE BURGER**

Thursday March 27

B ◀)) **7.01** **LISTEN FOR DETAIL** **Listen to the radio interviews again. Match the speakers with their opinions.**

1	Carol Saint Vincent	a	_____	"I think this is a delicious burger …"
2	Charles Davis	b	_____	"But mostly it tasted like some strange meat …"
3	Keila Summers	c	_____	"For me, it tasted amazing …"
4	Melissa Poitras	d	_____	"I'm so happy to write about this delicious burger."

2 READING

A **Read the food blog below. Then circle the correct answers.**

Burgers that taste like meat, but have no meat in them, are an amazing idea. Of course, they're also good for the health of both people and the planet. But most of us don't change our eating habits for food that tastes the same. It has to taste better! For example, some people in New York love the Best Burger, made by Dave Simmons, a popular chef. His grilled burger is made of cereal and mushrooms. It doesn't taste like meat, but it is really delicious. What do you think? Is the future of food all about science, or is it about what the customer wants?

1 The writer thinks that burgers with no meat are _____
  a the future of food   b a bad habit   c a great idea

2 The writer thinks that burgers without meat need to _____
  a be more popular than meat   b taste better than meat   c taste like meat

3 The Best Burger is _____
  a raw   b grilled   c fresh

4 What is the Best Burger mostly made of?
  a salmon   b meat   c mushrooms

WRITING

A   **Complete the interview. Use the expressions in the box.**

for me	my point of view	think	you ask me

Professor, you were the first person to make a "no-meat" burger in a science center. What do you think is the next step?

"From ¹_____, it's all about helping the planet. A few months ago, someone asked me: 'Can you do this with chicken?' If ²_____, that is an interesting idea. I ³_____ there are always many ways to find answers to a problem: for example, people can just eat less chicken, but we know they will not. ⁴_____, what is important is to answer a real problem, not to make new foods for the market."

B   **Read the professor's opinion again. Do you agree or disagree with his comments? Why?**
    What is your idea to help the planet? Write a blog post and explain your point of view.

CHECK AND REVIEW

Read the statements. Can you do these things?

UNIT 7	Mark the boxes. ☑ I can do it. [?] I am not sure. I can …	If you are not sure, go back to these pages in the Student's Book.
VOCABULARY	☐ use food vocabulary. ☐ use words to describe food.	page 66 page 68
GRAMMAR	☐ use quantifiers to talk about amounts. ☐ use verb patterns to say what I like.	page 67 page 69
FUNCTIONAL LANGUAGE	☐ order food and take food orders. ☐ use *I mean* to give more details.	page 70 page 71
SKILLS	☐ write a comment about an online article. ☐ give my opinion.	page 73 page 73

1 VOCABULARY: Traveling

A **Cross out the word that is different.**

1 tourists	tour guide	~~check-in counter~~
2 backpack	luggage	tour bus
3 backpack	check-in counter	suitcase
4 bus station	flight details	airplane
5 guidebooks	maps	tour guide

2 GRAMMAR: *if* and *when*

A **Match the two halves of the sentences.**

1 When I stay in hotels, …

2 When I only have one suitcase, …

3 When I arrive at the airport, …

4 When we take a tour bus, …

5 If I'm in a city for the first time, …

a _____ I find the check-in counter first.

b _____ I always bring a map to know where I am.

c _____ I always sleep late.

d _____ we always see a lot of the city.

e _____ I don't usually check my luggage.

B   **Use the information in the chart to write complete sentences.**

If / When	Situation	Option
When	Kim travels to Hawaii	stay near the beach
If	Matt flies internationally	travel first class
When	we visit a new town	try the food
If	they plan a trip	use guidebooks to get ideas
When	I go on a bus tour	bring my camera with me

1 _____

2 _____

3 _____

4 _____

5 _____

3   GRAMMAR AND VOCABULARY

A   **Use the information in the chart to write questions using *if* or *when*.**

Situation	Option 1	Option 2
travel abroad	bring one suitcase	bring more than one suitcase
have free time	visit new places	do nothing and stay home
go sightseeing	bring a guidebook	bring a map
go hiking	travel with a suitcase	travel with a backpack
go on vacation	meet new people	spend time with friends

1   *When you travel abroad, do you bring one suitcase or more than one suitcase?*

2 _____

3 _____

4 _____

5 _____

B   **Answer the questions in exercise A with your own information.**

1 _____

2 _____

3 _____

4 _____

5 _____

1 VOCABULARY: Using transportation

A **Find the words from the box in the word search.**

catch	change	drop off	get into
get off	get on	~~get out of~~	miss
pick up	take		

2 GRAMMAR: Giving reasons using *to* and *for*

A (Circle) **the correct answers to complete the sentences.**

1 Lauren is changing trains *for* / *to* get to her office.
2 We are stopping at the next town *for* / *to* breakfast.
3 I'm going into the bus station *for* / *to* buy a ticket.
4 They took a different flight *for* / *to* spend more time in San Francisco.
5 Sam picked him up *for* / *to* lunch.

G	E	T	O	F	F	P	T	D	D	M
G	E	T	O	U	T	O	F	R	V	I
X	B	Q	I	P	F	L	D	O	I	S
F	O	M	C	G	L	G	U	P	R	S
F	P	P	V	H	U	O	Z	O	G	D
C	E	I	R	B	A	A	L	F	E	B
A	L	F	C	O	G	N	R	F	T	G
T	A	G	T	K	P	E	G	P	I	E
C	D	E	J	C	U	O	C	E	N	T
H	G	M	H	A	S	P	Z	F	T	O
J	U	T	A	K	E	Y	A	D	O	N

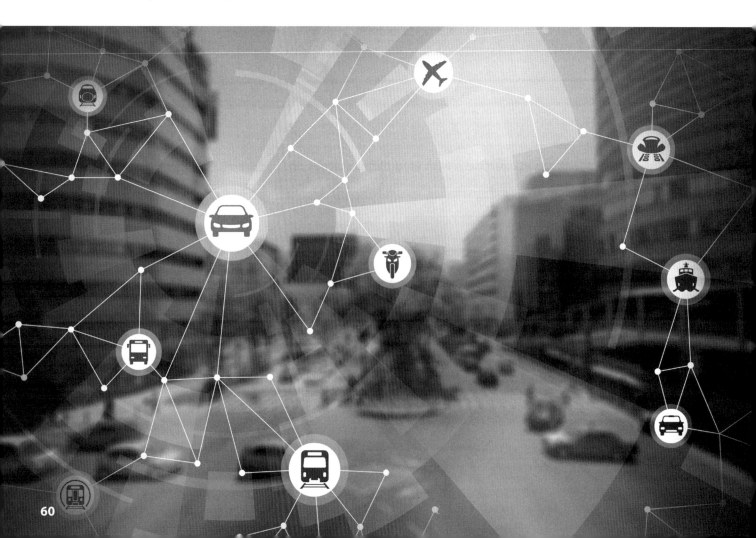

B Complete the travel blog with *for* or *to*.

TRIP OF A LIFETIME

I'm at the airport in Guadalajara. We're getting ready ¹_____ our trip to Monterrey. I'm looking at a map of the city ²_____ find our hotel. It's not far from *Barrio Antiguo*. When we get there, we plan to take a taxi, check in to the hotel, leave our suitcases in the room, and go out ³_____ dinner.

They're calling on the passengers to board the plane. Julia is buying some snacks ⁴_____ the flight, because they don't give us food on the plane. I'm getting in line ⁵_____ be one of the first people to board. I'm looking in my bag ⁶_____ find my ticket. Here it is!

3 GRAMMAR AND VOCABULARY

A Choose the correct answers about transportation.

1 My friend and I drive together to work. She _____ in the mornings.
   a takes a bus   b picks me up   c rides a train

2 We can't fly straight from here to Mexico City. We _____ in Miami.
   a change planes   b get out   c miss the flight

3 When I'm late, I _____ a taxi. It's faster.
   a get on   b pick up   c take

4 My friend drives a school bus. He _____ off the kids at school every morning.
   a drops   b gets   c takes

5 This traffic is so bad. I hope I don't _____ my plane.
   a catch   b change   c miss

B Write about a trip you took when you used different types of transportation.

_____

_____

_____

_____

THAT'S A GREAT IDEA!

1 FUNCTIONAL LANGUAGE: Giving advice and making suggestions

A Write the phrases from the box in the correct category.

| how about going | perfect | that would be great | that's a great idea |
| why don't you go | ~~you could take a taxi~~ | you should take | |

Making suggestions	Agreeing
you could take a taxi	

2 REAL-WORLD STRATEGY: Echo questions

A Complete the conversation using the echo questions in the box.

| how long | how often | what time | where |

A Here's your key. Breakfast starts at 7:00 a.m. tomorrow.

B Sorry, ¹_____?

A At 7:00 a.m. Is there anything else I can do for you?

B Yes, please. I need to be downtown at 10:00 a.m. tomorrow.

A Sorry, you are going ²_____?

B Downtown.

A A shuttle leaves from the hotel and goes downtown every hour.

B The shuttle leaves ³_____?

A Every hour.

B Thanks. And, how long does it take to get downtown?

A Usually about 30 minutes.

B I'm sorry, it takes ⁴_____?

A About 30 minutes.

B Great! Thanks so much.

3 FUNCTIONAL LANGUAGE AND REAL-WORLD STRATEGY

A   **Match the conversation with the correct response.**

1   I need to get to the airport tomorrow at 4:00 p.m.

2   It takes about 40 minutes to get there.

3   Where can I get souvenirs around here?

4   You need to take a taxi. It's faster.

5   Why don't you go to Brio? It's a great Italian restaurant in the mall.

a   Excuse me, how long?

b   Well, how about going to the mall around the corner?

c   That's a great idea. I don't want to be late.

d   Sorry, when did you say, sir?

e   Perfect! Where's the mall?

B   **Continue the conversation below.**

A   Where can I get souvenirs around here?

B   _____

A   _____

B   _____

A   _____

B   _____

A   _____

B   _____

A   _____

B   _____

A   _____

B   _____

A   _____

B   _____

LEAVING HOME

1 LISTENING

A 🔊 **8.01** Listen to a radio show and some answers to problems international students often have in the United States. Number the advice in the order you hear it.

_____ find a better home

_____ learn the language

_____ get to know people

_____ find out about the holidays

_____ find out about transportation

2 READING

A **Read the script, and ⊘circle⊘ the correct answers.**

▶ **Your**video   Profile   Channels   Sign out

Hi! I'm Silvie. Thanks for watching my Yourvideo channel. Many of you asked me to make a video about things that we international students at American colleges need to know. Well, here's my answer.

Here are five students from other countries giving advice on things every foreign student should know about living in the US for the first time.

Keila: If your flight is more than ten hours, you may feel tired the first week of class. So bring lots of water and coffee to school.

João: Make friends before vacation starts. Everybody goes home, and you don't want to be alone at school watching everyone's social media sites. Believe me.

Farid: Don't be surprised by how much food they give you here. Remember, it's a lot, but the food is delicious, too!

Antonio: It's OK if you don't know much about popular movies or art. You can always laugh a little and look it up later on the internet.

Kim: It's OK if you don't talk to your parents every day, because when they are up during the day and free to call you, you're not!

Let me just say, don't worry too much and have fun! Let me know what you think. And if you like the video – sign up!

---

1 Who made this video?

   a a teacher   **b** a student   **c** a parent

2 After a long trip, it's normal to feel _____ the first days of school.

   a tired   **b** surprised   **c** worried

3 Why should people make friends before vacation?

   a So they can ask for help.   **b** So they are not alone during vacation.

   c So they can study together.

4 For some students, it's normal not to talk to their parents every day because of _____.

   a food differences   **b** time differences   **c** language differences

5 What advice does Silvie give at the end of her video?

   a don't be alone   **b** study hard   **c** don't worry

3   WRITING

A   **Read the comments by the international students again. Write responses to them. Use the phrases in the box.**

> How about …   I really like the idea of …
> I think it's a good idea …   I think it's also very important …
> That's a great idea!   You could also offer …

To Keila:

I think it's a good idea to drink lots of water
when you feel tired after a long flight.

To Antonio:

To João:

To Kim:

To Farid:

B   **Write suggestions for international students at your school or in your hometown. What advice can you give them?**

CHECK AND REVIEW

Read the statements. Can you do these things?

UNIT 8	Mark the boxes. ✔ I can do it. ? I am not sure. **I can …**	If you are not sure, go back to these pages in the Student's Book.
VOCABULARY	☐ use words related to traveling. ☐ use verbs to talk about transportation.	page 76 page 78
GRAMMAR	☐ use *if* and *when* to talk about travel preferences. ☐ use *to* and *for* to give reasons.	page 77 page 79
FUNCTIONAL LANGUAGE	☐ give advice and make suggestions. ☐ use echo questions to ask for repetition.	page 80 page 81
SKILLS	☐ write a comment giving advice. ☐ use specific phrases to give advice.	page 83 page 83

UNIT 9 — LOOKING GOOD

9.1 WHAT TO WEAR AT WORK

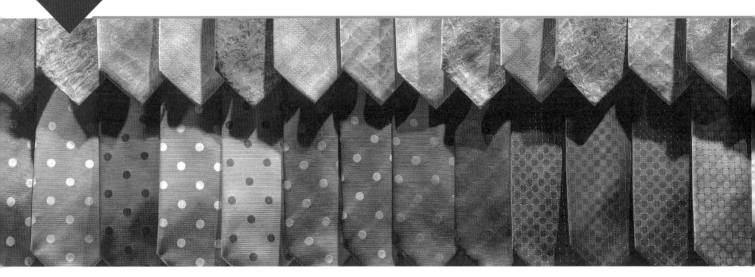

1 VOCABULARY: Naming accessories

A **Match the accessories to their uses.**

1	scarf	a	_____	wear on your hands
2	socks	b	_____	hang from your ears
3	earrings	c	_____	wear on your arm
4	gloves	d	_____	holds your pants up
5	sunglasses	e	_____	hang from your neck
6	belt	f	_1_	cover your neck
7	sneakers	g	_____	wear with a suit
8	bracelets	h	_____	cover your eyes
9	necklace	i	_____	cover your feet
10	tie	j	_____	wear to play basketball

2 GRAMMAR: Comparative adjectives

A **Write the adjectives under the correct category.**

~~attractive~~	cheap	cold	cool	expensive
friendly	important	interesting	warm	

More	-er
attractive	

66

B **Circle the correct words to complete the sentences.**

1 I wear *attractiver / more attractive* jewelry when I go to the theater.
2 That jacket is *more warm / warmer* than this one.
3 It's not possible to know if one person is *more interesting / interestinger* than another one.
4 That car is more expensive *that / than* my truck.
5 People are *more nice / nicer* around here.
6 Food at this store is *cheaper / more cheap* than at that other store.

3 GRAMMAR AND VOCABULARY

A **Complete the sentences based on the information in the chart. Each accessory is rated from 1–5. Five is the highest score.**

	Gloves	Earrings	Necklaces	Scarves	Socks
price	✓✓✓	✓✓✓✓	✓✓✓✓✓	✓✓✓	✓✓
warm	✓✓✓✓	✓	✓	✓✓✓	✓✓✓
fashionable	✓✓✓	✓✓✓✓	✓✓✓✓✓	✓✓✓	✓
quality	✓✓✓	✓✓✓✓✓	✓✓✓✓	✓✓✓✓	✓✓✓✓
importance	✓✓✓✓	✓✓✓	✓✓	✓	✓✓✓✓✓
attractive	✓✓	✓✓✓	✓✓✓	✓✓✓	✓

1 Necklaces are more important than _____scarves_____ .
2 Earrings are more fashionable than _____.
3 Gloves are cheaper than _____.
4 Scarves are better quality than _____.
5 _____ are more attractive than socks.
6 _____ are warmer than scarves.

B **Write similar comparisons using the other information in exercise A.**

_____   _____
_____   _____
_____   _____

67

9.2 BABY PHOTOS

1 VOCABULARY: Describing appearance

A **Look at the clues, and complete the crossword.**

Across:

b …

p … e …

m …

l …. hair

Down:

c … g … hair

b …

d … s … hair

2 GRAMMAR: Superlative adjectives

A **Use superlatives to complete the sentences.**

1 It is a very nice room. It is the _____ _nicest_ _____ in the hotel.

2 It is a very cheap restaurant. It is the _____ in town.

3 I am so happy. It is the _____ day of my life.

4 It's a very expensive painting. It is the _____ in the art show.

5 Spring is a very busy time for me. It is the _____ time of the year.

6 This is a very difficult class. It is the _____ class I have right now.

B   **Complete the sentences with the correct form of the adjectives in parentheses.**

   1 We stayed at the _____cheapest_____ (cheap) hotel in town.
   2 The United States is very large, but Russia is the _____ (large) country in the world.
   3 We had a great time. It was one of the _____ (amazing) vacations of our lives.
   4 He is the _____ (famous) actor in movies today.
   5 It's so hot out there! This is the _____ (warm) day of the summer.
   6 These shoes are the _____ (fashionable) shoes of this season.

3 GRAMMAR AND VOCABULARY

A   **Think about your friends, family, and famous people. Write the name of a person who …**

is tall / in your family	
has curly hair / family or friend	
dresses nice / in your school	
has beautiful eyes / a famous person	
has a beard / person you know	
looks good with a mustache	

B   **Use superlative adjectives to write sentences about the information from exercise A.**

   1 _____
   2 _____
   3 _____
   4 _____
   5 _____
   6 _____

9.3 WHAT DO YOU THINK OF THIS?

1 FUNCTIONAL LANGUAGE: Asking for opinions

A **Write the phrases in the correct category.**

> Do you think it's kind of bright?
> I guess.
> Isn't it nice?
> It's perfect.
>
> ~~Do you like it?~~
> I'm not sure.
> I think this one doesn't match.
> What do you think of it?
>
> How do you feel about it?
> I prefer the other one.
> It looks bad.

Asking for an opinion	Positive opinion	Negative or neutral opinion
Do you like it?		

2 REAL-WORLD STRATEGY: Giving opinions; *I guess*

A **Complete the sentences. Use the phrases in the box above to help you. Then match the question to the best answer.**

1 Are these gloves fashionable?
I'm _____not sure_____.

2 Let me try the white pair. What _____ of these?

3 How _____ about leather gloves?

4 _____ I could try a green pair. Do you like green?

5 Those blue gloves are the same color as my blouse. _____! What do you think?

a _____ Hmm. I'm not sure. Isn't white a little formal?

b _____ It looks nice, but don't you think green is kind of bright?

c __1__ Well, a lot more people are wearing them now.

d _____ Oh, yes! Those go well with your blouse.

e _____ They're not bad, but do you think leather is kind of expensive?

3 FUNCTIONAL LANGUAGE AND REAL-WORLD STRATEGY

A   **Look at the pictures and write a conversation about one pair of sneakers. Use the phrases in the box.**

Do you like them?	Don't you think … ?	How do you feel about … ?	I guess …
I prefer …	I think these are …	I'm not sure.	They look …
They're perfect.	What do you think of … ?		

1 A *What do you think of those sneakers?*

   B

   A

   B

2 A

   B

   A

   B

3 A

   B

   A

   B

1 READING: Asking for opinions

A **Read the following text that describes an advertisement and circle the correct answers.**

> A young man with sunglasses and expensive clothes is driving a blue car.
> The car is driving very fast on a beautiful open road, in the woods.
> Now there is a second car. It's red. Both cars want to be the first one to
> get to the next town. The driver in the blue car arrives in the town first.
> He gets out of the car and laughs. It's a beautiful day and he feels happy.

1 The advertisement is selling _____.
  a vacations   **b** sunglasses   **c** cars

2 It is a _____ ad.
  a TV   **b** radio   **c** magazine

3 In the ad, what is the most important idea about the car?
  a what color it is   **b** how fast it goes   **c** how big it is

4 Who is the advertisement selling to?
  a families   **b** teenagers   **c** adults

5 What is the message behind the advertisement?
  a Blue is better than red.   **b** This is the best car to buy.   **c** It is good to be a safe driver.

2 LISTENING

A 🔊 **9.01** **Listen to the radio advertisement and circle the correct words to complete the sentences.**

1 The advertisement is about a special *model car / car sale*.

2 The car company has *hundreds / thousands* of cars to sell.

3 The sale will last for only a *weekend / a week*.

4 The sale price is *half / hundreds* off the regular price.

5 The company has *only a few / many different* types of cars to choose from.

6 The company is waiting for you to *take home a car / see their car show*.

B 🔊 **9.01** **Listen to the radio advertisement again. Does the advertisement make you want to go there? Write about why you do or don't want to buy a car from this company.**

_____

_____

_____

3 WRITING

A **Rewrite the advertisement text using the correct punctuation and capitalization.**

when everythings in the right place you cant go wrong thats why the newest model from August Car Company makes it easy to choose the August Classic you can drive it in the city or you can take it on the open road you can seat up to eight people in it and feel safe its the perfect way to get comfortable with the new science behind today's cars this is the new August Classic.

its your kind of car learn more at August.com

B **Write the text for an advertisement based on the following product description.**

- The Lemon 16.4 is the most useful car of all time.
- The Lemon is the smallest city car with two doors. It is only 8.5 feet long.
- You can easily drive up to two people, and you can park almost anywhere. It is the perfect mix of space and size.
- The Lemon comes in many colors – black, red, and blue. It costs less than other cars on the market.

CHECK AND REVIEW

Read the statements. Can you do these things?

UNIT 9	Mark the boxes. ☑ I can do it. ? I am not sure. **I can ...**	If you are not sure, go back to these pages in the Student's Book.
VOCABULARY	☐ use words for fashion accessories. ☐ talk about people's appearance.	page 86 page 88
GRAMMAR	☐ compare things using adjectives. ☐ use superlative adjectives.	page 87 page 89
FUNCTIONAL LANGUAGE	☐ ask for, and give, an opinion. ☐ use *I guess* when I'm not sure.	page 90 page 91
SKILLS	☐ write a commercial. ☐ use uppercase letters, punctuation, and contraction apostrophes.	page 93 page 93

UNIT 10 RISKY BUSINESS

10.1 DANGER ON THE JOB

1 VOCABULARY: Describing jobs

A Find the words in the box in the word search.

accountant	architect	call center worker	dentist
engineer	IT specialist	lawyer	mechanic
nurse	paramedic	photographer	physical therapist
police officer	project manager	receptionist	

P	P	H	Y	S	I	C	A	L	T	H	E	R	A	P	I	S	T
R	P	H	O	T	O	G	R	A	P	H	E	R	O	V	R	F	V
O	F	K	D	I	M	E	C	H	A	N	I	C	R	T	X	S	J
J	E	P	A	R	A	M	E	D	I	C	P	E	K	P	T	F	C
E	B	G	G	P	J	C	R	E	F	V	B	R	G	M	I	I	P
C	D	G	I	K	L	T	R	U	C	A	P	F	C	C	T	X	A
T	B	U	O	F	M	L	E	S	N	W	L	F	S	A	S	V	C
M	I	F	X	Z	L	J	C	I	R	C	A	D	V	R	P	O	C
A	W	V	K	G	L	O	E	F	E	P	W	Z	E	C	E	N	O
N	R	A	X	S	K	T	P	V	N	A	Y	A	H	H	C	U	U
A	Q	X	N	T	C	N	T	C	G	M	E	K	L	I	I	R	N
G	P	U	R	U	U	D	I	H	I	O	R	H	E	T	A	S	T
E	G	V	J	C	I	K	O	G	N	P	U	J	F	E	L	E	A
R	S	O	L	L	G	Z	N	H	E	Z	O	B	T	C	I	B	N
I	R	L	A	M	L	X	I	R	E	Y	Q	O	V	T	S	N	T
L	O	D	E	N	T	I	S	T	R	I	E	Y	C	W	T	K	G
C	A	L	L	C	E	N	T	E	R	W	O	R	K	E	R	F	G
Q	U	P	O	L	I	C	E	O	F	F	I	C	E	R	W	U	Z

2 GRAMMAR: *have to*

A Use *have / has* to and the best verb to complete the sentence. Use the negative when necessary.

1 Mechanics _____ *have to repair* _____ cars.

2 A photographer _____ a camera.

3 A paramedic _____ inside a hospital.

4 An accountant _____ numbers.

5 Dentists _____ people with broken legs.

6 Call center workers _____ on the telephone.

74

B **Correct the sentences below.**

1 What kind of emergencies you have to help with?

   What kind of emergencies do you have to help with?

2 I haven't to write a new software program.

3 A receptionist hasn't to stand up all day.

4 When have photographers to talk to actors?

5 Call center workers haven't to make long business calls.

6 Do you have to doing anything dangerous in your work?

---

3 GRAMMAR AND VOCABULARY

A **Look at the information in the schedule. Write sentences about what the restaurant staff has to do each day.**

	Mon	Tue	Wed
Paul (server)	Serve food	Serve drinks and dessert	Serve food
Ray (chef)	Test new desserts	Write a new dinner menu	Buy vegetables and meat
Sam (owner)	Send emails to customers	Write a new dinner menu	Hire new server
Mica (server)	Serve food	Welcome customers	Serve food

1 *Paul and Mica have to serve food on Monday and Wednesday.*

2

3

4

5

75

DON'T WORRY, DAD

1 VOCABULARY: Describing health problems

A **Choose the correct verb to complete the sentence. Change the verb into the simple past.**

1 I _____ (break / cut) my finger with a knife.

2 I _____ (catch /feel) a cold. I'm sneezing a lot.

3 I _____ (break / twist) my leg when I was on vacation.

4 I _____ (have / feel) stressed last week. I had too much work.

5 I fell over yesterday and _____ (twist / cut) my ankle. Now I can't walk.

6 Ouch! I just _____ (bang / break) my head on the desk.

7 I _____ (have / catch) a headache when I woke up this morning.

8 I _____ (catch / have) a fever last week. I stayed home for 3 days.

2 GRAMMAR: Making predictions

A **Complete the sentences with the words in the box.**

may	maybe	might	probably	will	won't

1 I have to return the book I borrowed, so I _____ go to the library tomorrow.

2 I think she _____ be OK.

3 I'm not sure, but _____ he won't win the race. The other runners are very fast.

4 With all those courses, I think you will _____ feel very stressed at the end of the year.

5 I _____ fail this exam. I studied hard, so I know for sure that I will pass this time!

6 I _____ not be the best-looking person, but I'm the best actor.

B Write the phrases from the box in the correct category.

Do you think	I'll probably	It might be	Maybe it'll	Perhaps
What will	Will this	Will you	Won't	You'll

Ask about the future	Express future possibility	Express future plans

3 GRAMMAR AND VOCABULARY

A Read the situations and make predictions about them using the language from exercise 2B.

1 Bobby has a cold. He didn't study enough and feels very stressed about the math test.
   Bobby might not pass his test.

2 Many couples are having babies today. The hospital is already full, and Dr. Mills has a very busy morning.
   _____

3 Angela woke up late. She cut her finger making breakfast. She has to go to the doctor.
   _____

4 Kevin twisted his ankle at basketball practice. The final game of the year is tomorrow. His team needs him for the game.
   _____

5 Eva had a job interview yesterday. She was late, and she wore sneakers and jeans.
   _____

6 It's Lara's birthday today. She asked her parents for a dog. Last night she heard strange noises in the yard.
   _____

7 Marco is walking home in the rain. He forgot his umbrella, and missed the bus.
   _____

8 Daniel bought a ring for his girlfriend. Tonight he's taking her to a romantic restaurant for dinner.
   _____

10.3 WHAT'S THE MATTER?

1 FUNCTIONAL LANGUAGE: Describing a medical problem and asking for help

A **Label the phrases according to their use: (O) offering help, (I) asking for information, (H) asking someone for help, or (S) describing symptoms.**

1 What's wrong?   I
2 My chest hurts.
3 Can you get me my medicine?
4 How can I help?
5 I need a towel.
6 What's the matter?

7 It hurts to walk.
8 I have a pain in my back.
9 Should I call a doctor?
10 What happened?
11 What do you want me to do?
12 Where exactly does it hurt?

2 REAL-WORLD STRATEGY: *It's like / It feels like*

A **Find <u>three</u> places in the conversation where you can use *It's like* or *It feels like*.**

A How can I help you today?
B I don't feel well. My head is killing me.
A How strong is your headache?
B Someone is hitting my head with a book.
A How do your eyes feel?

B They hurt. My eyes are on fire.
A Any other symptoms?
B My fingers are numb. I don't have my fingers.
A OK, let me look at you.

3 FUNCTIONAL LANGUAGE AND REAL-WORLD STRATEGY

A Look at the pictures. Write a caption for each situation. Use an expression that matches the text in parentheses.

(Offering help)

(Asking for information about the problem)

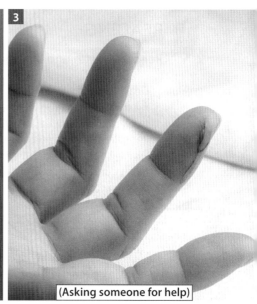

(Asking someone for help)

How can I help you?

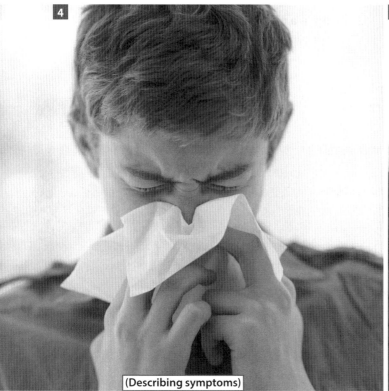

(Describing symptoms)

(Offering help)

10.4 FACE YOUR FEARS

1 READING

A **Read the letter and answer the questions.**

> Dear Max,
>
> I'm the teaching program manager, and we are excited to have you join us. Tomorrow you'll fly to South Africa! For two years, you will stay in a village near Cape Town. You'll teach the children in the small school there. This work is very important, so be proud of yourself. Very few people spend two years of their lives after college helping poor people. You will be away from home for a long time, so you might want to bring some music and books. And you're going to miss your family, so bring photos. It's important to remember them. Also, don't forget your medicine, you will need it. I'll meet you at the airport in Cape Town in a few days. Please email me any time you have questions.
>
> Good luck!
>
> Tom Princeton

1 Who is writing this letter?
   a Max's teacher   **b** Max's relative   **c** Max's boss

2 Where is Max going?
   a Europe   **b** Asia   **c** Africa

3 What is Max doing for the next two years?
   a studying   **b** teaching   **c** sightseeing

4 What should Max be ready for?
   a missing his family   **b** working a lot   **c** living in a city

2 LISTENING

A 🔊 **10.01** **Listen to the video message and number the sentences or paragraphs in the order you hear them.**

Welcome!

_____ Please read the files and documents that our staff gave you.

_____ Finally, I'll be available to answer all the questions you might have.

_____ I'm the manager of the Helping Hands program for this country.

_____ Good luck, and enjoy your time here!

_____ I want to thank you for coming. Our team is very excited to have you with us.

_____ But you have to stay healthy.

_____ Tomorrow you will start working at our medical station.

_____ The work you will do in the next few weeks is very important, but it is also dangerous. Many people need our help.

_____ Please remember to have your ID and your cell phone with you at all times.

B 🔊 **10.01** Listen to the video message again and write the number of each sentence in the correct category.

Introduction	Giving advice	Positive ending

3 WRITING

A **Complete the email with your own answers. Add** *anyway* **and** *by the way.*

● ● ●   Reply Forward ✉

Hey Ivan,

My name is ¹_____, and I heard you are joining our English class. That's great.
²_____, the ³_____ is excellent and the class is really fun.
⁴_____, you've missed two lessons, so, let me give you some advice about
the things we did in those classes. The last topic we covered was ⁵_____.
For homework, ⁶_____.
During class, ⁷_____.
After class, ⁸_____.
I hope this helps you have a good start. Let me know if you have any other questions.
Take care,
⁹_____

CHECK AND REVIEW

Read the statements. Can you do these things?

UNIT 10	Mark the boxes. ☑ I can do it. ❓ I am not sure. **I can …**	If you are not sure, go back to these pages in the Student's Book.
VOCABULARY	☐ use words to describe jobs. ☐ use words to describe health problems.	page 98 page 100
GRAMMAR	☐ use *have to* to talk about things that are necessary. ☐ make predictions about the future with *will*.	page 99 page 101
FUNCTIONAL LANGUAGE	☐ describe a medical problem and ask for help. ☐ use *it's like* and *it feels like* to describe a problem.	page 102 page 103
SKILLS	☐ write a letter of advice. ☐ use *anyway* and *by the way*.	page 105 page 105

11.1   I'VE NEVER BEEN HAPPIER!

1 VOCABULARY: Using verb-noun internet phrases

A   Write ten verb-noun phrases with the words below.

add someone	a	app
build	an	friend
change	as a	group
check	on a	link
click	your	messages
join		social media account
make		password
message		right
open		someone
swipe		video

1 add someone as a friend
2 _____
3 _____
4 _____
5 _____

6 _____
7 _____
8 _____
9 _____
10 _____

2 GRAMMAR: Present perfect for experience

A   Complete the chart with the present perfect form of the verbs.

Simple present	Present perfect
be	have been
build	
do	
have	
join	
make	
message	

B   **Correct the sentences.**

1   She have build hundreds of websites. _____

2   Have you ever were to Japan? _____

3   Has they change their passwords? _____

4   I don't have checked my messages. _____

5   He have added me as a friend. _____

3   GRAMMAR AND VOCABULARY

A   **Write questions using present perfect. Use the answers to help you.**

1   A   *Have you ever been outside the country?*
    B   No, I've never been outside the country.

2   A   _____
    B   No, they've never built an app.

3   A   _____
    B   Yes, I've made two videos with my friends.

4   A   _____
    B   No, I've never added someone I don't know as a friend.

5   A   _____
    B   No, she's never messaged a famous person.

6   A   _____
    B   Yes, he has changed his password!

7   A   _____
    B   Yes, she's written three songs.

8   A   _____
    B   Yes, they've lived in a different country.

9   A   _____
    B   No, he hasn't found a job.

10 A   _____
    B   Yes, I've checked my messages.

1 VOCABULARY: Using social media verbs

A Make words from the letters.

1 dloadwno ___download___
2 wollfo _____
3 agilorv _____
4 rkmoobak _____
5 olpuda _____

6 rofacehrs _____
7 iekl _____
8 kcobl _____
9 nigol _____
10 arshe _____

B (Circle) the correct options to complete the sentences.

1 Have you ever *uploaded / gone viral* photos of your friends to a social media site?
2 Catherine *searched / followed* for a new coat online.
3 The video of Paula and Rajesh's wedding party *liked / went viral*. You have to see the dancing!
4 Last night I *blocked / downloaded* the English class assignment. I needed to study it.
5 Have you ever *logged in / shared* to that website where you can see your house?
6 There is a problem with that website. I tried to open it, but my computer *blocked / liked* it.

2 GRAMMAR: Present perfect and simple past

A Read the sentences. Then write a question about each one in the simple past.

1 I've downloaded this great app.   When ___did you download it___ ?
2 I've uploaded some photos onto my Facebook page.   When _____ ?
3 She's blocked her ex-boyfriend.   Why _____ ?
4 I've lost my phone.   Where _____ ?
5 We've met so many interesting people.   Where _____ ?
6 He's found an old friend from ten years ago on Facebook.   How _____ ?

B   **Complete the text with the correct form of the verbs in parentheses. Look up the past participle of the verbs if you need to.**

Have I ever [1] _____lost_____ (lose) my phone? Yes, I have. I [2] _____
(lose) it on the bus last week, but someone [3] _____ (find) it and I got it
back. But I [4] _____ (never break) my phone. My sister [5] _____
(break) three phones! The last time, she was in the kitchen and she [6] _____
(drop) it into the tomato sauce. She [7] _____ (clean) it, but it
didn't help. Yesterday, she [8] _____ (buy) her fourth phone.

3   GRAMMAR AND VOCABULARY

A   **Write questions using the verbs and phrases with the present perfect.**

1   (eat) most expensive restaurant   _What is the most expensive restaurant you've ever eaten in?_
2   (be) in a video   _____
3   (study) Japanese   _____
4   (walk) far in one day   _____
5   (forget) the birthday of someone important _____
6   (receive) best gift   _____
7   (take) funniest photo   _____
8   (cook) for a lot of people   _____

B   **Write your answers to the questions in exercise A.**

1   _Gina's Italian Restaurant in Rio is the most expensive restaurant I've ever eaten in._
2   _____
3   _____
4   _____
5   _____
6   _____
7   _____
8   _____

11.3 CAN I USE YOUR PHONE?

1 FUNCTIONAL LANGUAGE: Making and responding to requests

A Write the phrases in the box in the correct category.

Can I	Could you	I'm afraid not	No, I'm sorry
No problem	Would you mind	Yeah, that's fine	

Making requests	Accepting requests	Refusing requests

2 REAL-WORLD STRATEGY: Remembering words

A Complete the conversations using the questions in the box.

What do you call …	What do you call …	What's his/her …	What's it …

A Hi, do you need any help?

B Hi, yes. Do you mind taking a look at my … ¹ _____ called?

A Your tablet? No problem.

B Thanks. I downloaded a video yesterday, and now I can't open my …
² _____ it?

A Your email?

B Yes, my email. Could you take a look, please?

A Wow, she's beautiful! ³ _____ name?

B Her name is Felicity Jones.

A Is she a … ⁴ _____ it?

B An actor? Yes, she's a movie star.

A Awesome!

3 FUNCTIONAL LANGUAGE AND REAL-WORLD STRATEGY

A Read the situations below and choose one. You will write a conversation asking for help. Before you write the conversation, complete the chart with expressions you plan to use.

You are a tourist. Ask someone for a good restaurant in town.

You are lost in a new city. Ask someone to give you directions.

Asking someone to do something	
Accepting requests	
Refusing requests	
Remembering words	

B Write your conversation with the expressions from exercise A.

A Hi. _____ ?

B _____

A _____

B _____

A _____

B _____

A _____

B _____

11.4 SELFIES

1 READING

A **Read the magazine article. Then read the sentences and write *T* if true or *F* if false. Then write true sentences for the false ones.**

HOW TO TAKE AMAZING SELFIES!

Love to take selfies, but hate the way they look? Here are some simple tips to look your best and have amazing selfies!

TIP 1 Light is your most important friend. How often have your photos looked too dark? Could you go outside or stand near a window to take your selfie? That's much better. You'll look so beautiful!

TIP 2 What's behind you? Is it an exciting place or only your face? If you hold the camera too close, your nose looks very big! Can we fix that? No problem! Hold your phone far away, and use the zoom. Then your face will look normal.

TIP 3 Wear fun accessories like sunglasses, a big hat, or a scarf. Make your selfies interesting!

TIP 4 Laugh! Be happy and you'll have an amazing selfie!

1 _____ This article is about how to dress better.

2 _____ The article says it's difficult to take selfies outside.

3 _____ The article explains why your nose may look too big in selfies.

4 _____ The writer doesn't know how to solve the problem of big noses in selfies.

5 _____ The writer thinks wearing hats make selfies boring.

6 _____ The writer probably likes happy selfies best.

2 LISTENING

A 🔊 **11.01** **Listen to the conversation. Then ⃝circle the correct answers.**

1 Tanya is having a problem _____.
   a taking selfies　　　b fixing her camera　　　c using her social media site

2 How does Tanya describe her photos?
   a They're too light.　　　b They're all terrible.　　　c They're too dark.

3 What does Shin think will probably help Tanya's photos?
   a uploading them　　　b using the flash　　　c making them darker

4 What does Tanya ask Shin to do?
   a take photos of her　　　b take photos with her　　　c teach her how to take photos

B 🔊 **11.01** **Listen to the conversation again. Then complete the sentences with phrases from the conversation.**

1 I ___have taken___ so many selfies, and they're all terrible.

2 I've looked at the photos _____.

3 Have you used the _____ ?

4 I've _____ it.

5 Hey, _____ teaching me more about taking photos?

6 _____ Monday?

3 WRITING

A **Complete the sentences about you.**

1 I take selfies when _____

2 I never take selfies when _____

3 I share selfies with _____

4 I take selfies at _____

5 I change selfies when _____

B **Read the article about selfies again. What information is useful? Use your answers in exercise A to write about how you take selfies. Include something positive, something negative, and something that you had a different idea about before.**

_____

_____

_____

_____

CHECK AND REVIEW

Read the statements. Can you do these things?

UNIT 11	Mark the boxes. ☑ I can do it. ? I am not sure. I can …	If you are not sure, go back to these pages in the Student's Book.
VOCABULARY	☐ use verb-noun internet phrases.	page 108
	☐ use social media verbs.	page 110
GRAMMAR	☐ use the present perfect to talk about experience.	page 109
	☐ use the present perfect and simple past to talk about what I've done and when I did it.	page 111
FUNCTIONAL LANGUAGE	☐ make and respond to requests.	page 112
	☐ ask questions to remember words.	page 113
SKILLS	☐ write comments about an online article.	page 115
	☐ use *I always thought …, I think it's interesting that …,* and *Who cares?*	page 115

1 VOCABULARY: Describing weather

A   Look at the pictures and complete the crossword.

Across:

2   4   5

8   11   12

13   14

Down:

1   2   3

4   6   7

9   10

2 GRAMMAR: *be like*

A **Put the words in the correct order to make questions.**

1 the / like / What's / weather / ?
   What's the weather like?

2 course / like / will / be / the / What / ?

3 What / party / was / like / the /?

4 music / was / the / like / What / ?

5 she / younger / What / like / was / when / she / was / ?

6 be / What / the / will / teacher / like / ?

B **Match the questions in exercise A to the answers below.**

_____ The music was excellent.

_____ I heard he will be great.

__1__ It's sunny and warm.

_____ It will be hard because the textbook is very difficult.

_____ It was fun because a lot of friends came by.

_____ She was very funny and happy.

3 GRAMMAR AND VOCABULARY

A **Answer the questions with your own information. Write complete sentences.**

1 What's the weather like today?

2 What's your best friend like?

3 What was your last birthday party like?

4 What will this weekend be like for you?

5 What are your English classmates like?

THIS TRIP HAS IT ALL

1 VOCABULARY: Describing landscapes and cityscapes

A **Find the words from the box in the word search.**

cave	cliff	coast	fountain	glacier
rainforest	rocks	skyscraper	stadium	statue
stream	tower	valley	waterfall	

```
R  S  Y  R  M  I  E  L  D  Q  E  E  T  G
G  E  F  A  O  W  L  T  C  X  U  C  P  L
O  W  O  I  G  P  S  F  D  U  T  A  Y  A
X  A  U  N  M  F  H  T  J  O  A  V  C  C
D  T  N  F  A  Z  W  S  A  T  T  E  D  I
S  E  T  O  L  L  T  U  K  D  S  N  I  E
X  R  A  R  L  I  G  D  K  H  I  Z  X  R
J  F  I  E  S  T  R  E  A  M  D  U  G  F
Y  A  N  S  F  H  Y  R  H  R  W  L  M  E
B  L  G  T  S  K  Y  S  C  R  A  P  E  R
O  L  P  H  E  H  M  H  P  T  O  W  E  R
O  K  Q  T  T  C  L  I  F  F  D  F  N  Y
I  S  T  A  T  U  E  M  L  C  O  A  S  T
X  J  R  O  C  K  S  K  V  A  L  L  E  Y
```

B **Choose the correct answer.**

1 After a day of sightseeing in Rome, we sat by the _____ of a horse in front of the large skyscraper.

   a statue   **b** rocks   **c** waterfall

2 From the ship we could see the large white ice that formed the _____.

   a valley   **b** glacier   **c** skyscraper

3 You will often know a city when you see pictures of its _____.

   a streams   **b** rainforests   **c** skyscrapers

4 Acapulco is famous for its swimmers who jump from the _____.

   a cliffs   **b** caves   **c** towers

5 Thousands of people come to the _____ to see sports and concerts.

   a valley   **b** stadium   **c** cave

6 Some people enjoy walking through a _____ to catch fish.

   a stream   **b** coast   **c** fountain

2 GRAMMAR: Relative pronouns: *who, which, that*

A **Complete the sentences with *who, which,* or *that*.**

1 The person _____*who*_____ helps you at the store is the clerk.

2 This is the song _____ my parents danced to at their wedding.

3 This is the painting _____ makes me feel calm.

4 Those are the people _____ I spend more time with.

5 This is my friend _____ always helps when I'm in trouble.

6 It is a city _____ is fun day and night.

B **Correct the sentences.**

1 That's the person which helped me last time.

_____

2 That's the jacket who I wear almost every day.

_____

3 Those are the presents who I received last month.

_____

4 It is one place who I would really like to visit in the future.

_____

5 That's the player which scored more points in the game.

_____

3 GRAMMAR AND VOCABULARY

A **Answer the questions with your own information. Write complete sentences.**

1 Who is your friend who likes to take photos?
Jacques is a friend who likes to take photos.

_____

2 What's the TV show that you watch every day?

_____

3 What's the last book that you read?

_____

4 What's the video game which you like the most?

_____

5 What's the city that you want to visit next?

_____

6 What's the sport that you play the most?

_____

1   FUNCTIONAL LANGUAGE: Asking for help and giving directions

A   **Put the conversation in order.**

- [ ] Luigi's? No, you need to go back the way you came. See that store there?
- [1] Hello, excuse me. We're looking for Luigi's Restaurant. Are we going in the right direction?
- [ ] Store? Oh, that one on the corner?
- [ ] Oh, dear. That's a long way.
- [ ] That's right! Turn right on that corner.
- [ ] OK, we turn right, and then what?
- [ ] Thanks. We'll try walking.
- [ ] Then walk for 15 minutes down the street, and you'll see Luigi's on the left.
- [ ] You can also take the bus on the corner. It comes every 30 minutes.

2   REAL-WORLD STRATEGY: Correcting yourself

A   **Use the words in the box to correct the statements.**

> No, wait …   Well, actually …

1   The Eiffel Tower is in New York City.   *Well, actually, the Eiffel Tower is in Paris.*
2   There is no water on Mars.
3   New Year's Eve is in June.
4   Tokyo is in Europe.
5   December is cold in Australia.

A   **Look at the map below and complete the conversations with the correct phrases.**

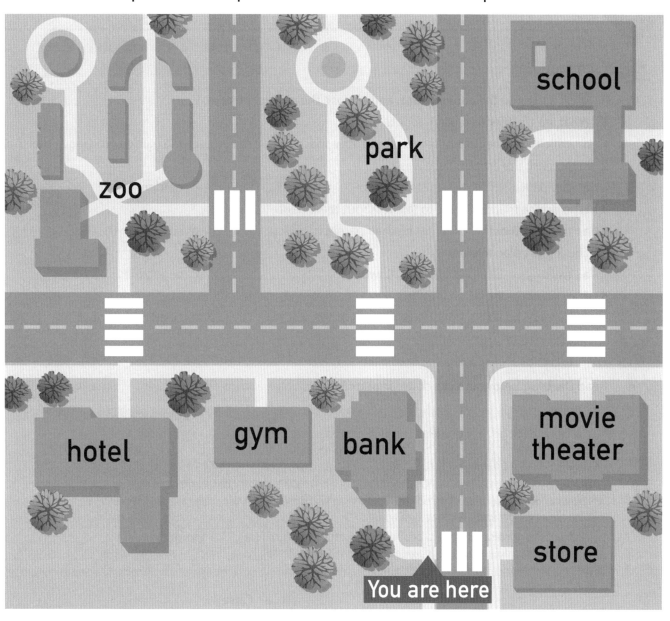

A

A Excuse me. ¹_____ us, please? ²_____
for the school.

B ³_____ (give directions). ⁴_____. (correct
yourself)

A OK. Can you show me on the map?

B ⁵_____. (positive response)

A Great, thanks!

B

A Excuse me, I'm looking for the hotel. ⁶_____?

B ⁷_____. (give directions, then correct yourself)

A Thanks!

GUERRILLA GARDENING

1 LISTENING

A 🔊 **12.01** **Listen to the conversation and choose the correct answer.**

1 What are the friends talking about?

   a which area they like best   b the empty space on the street   c the garden growing at their house

2 In the past, the empty space was a _____.

   a city park   b school   c garden

3 Who do the friends decide to talk to about their idea?

   a the neighbors   b their parents   c some farmers

4 The friends plan to plant _____.

   a trees   b flowers   c vegetables

5 They want to start a _____.

   a farmers' market   b grocery store   c cleaning business

2 READING

A **Read the blog below and check (✓) True or False.**

> I've never been good with plants, but I moved to a new apartment that's not very big, and decided I needed a wall garden. Why? Well, plants are beautiful to look at and they help clean the air. A wall garden is a way that a lot of plants can grow without taking too much floor space.
>
> It's not very easy to grow a wall garden. You have to make sure it's not too heavy, and that it gets enough light. Also, you have to make sure you don't give it too much water. Then the plants get yellow and their leaves fall off.
>
> The most important thing for a beautiful wall garden is plant food. Put some in the water every month, and you will have awesome green plants. It's the best thing I've ever done!

		True	False
1	Large plants will fit in the writer's apartment.	☐	☐
2	The writer has always been good with plants.	☐	☐
3	Wall gardens need good planning.	☐	☐
4	The most important thing is to water the plants very often.	☐	☐
5	The writer is happy with the garden.	☐	☐

3 WRITING

A **Use the words in the box to complete the instructions.**

> Finally   First   Next   Now   Then

Five Steps to Food from the Garden to Your Table: Grow Your Own Salad!

1 _____, go to your local store and buy seeds for lettuce, tomatoes, onions, and other salad favorites.

2 _____, make sure you have space for each type of plant.

3 _____, plant your seeds in a sunny place and water them twice a week.

4 _____ watch your plants grow.

5 _____, get your lettuce, a tomato, and an onion from the garden. Wash them, and enjoy your fresh salad!

B **Write five steps to selling your vegetables at a farmers' market. Use the phrases in the box.**

> choose the vegetables   get the vegetables from the garden   sell your vegetables
> wash the vegetables   write the price

1 _____

2 _____

3 _____

4 _____

5 _____

CHECK AND REVIEW

Read the statements. Can you do these things?

UNIT 12	Mark the boxes. ☑ I can do it. ? I am not sure.	If you are not sure, go back to these pages in the Student's Book.
	I can ...	
VOCABULARY	☐ use words to describe the weather.	page 118
	☐ use words to talk about landscapes and cityscapes.	page 120
GRAMMAR	☐ ask and answer questions with *be like*.	page 119
	☐ use *who, which,* and *that* to give information about people and things.	page 121
FUNCTIONAL LANGUAGE	☐ ask for help and give directions.	page 122
	☐ correct myself.	page 123
SKILLS	☐ write simple, short instructions.	page 125
	☐ use sequencing words.	page 125

EXTRA ACTIVITIES

7 TIME TO SPEAK The perfect party

A **Design the menu you created in class for your party. Use your own ideas, or you can find ideas online. Complete the fields with the necessary information.**
- date
- event name
- menu dishes
- descriptions of the dishes

B **Find pictures of your dishes. Illustrate the menu with the pictures.**

C **Bring your menu to the next class. Show it and explain it to the rest of the class.**

8 TIME TO SPEAK Planning a trip

A **Help tourists plan their trip by writing a review for a travel website.**
- Think of a place you have visited.
- List the things you did and the places you visited there.
- Write one comment for each place or activity based on your experience.
- In each comment, make one suggestion for other travelers.
- Go to a travel website.
- Find the places on your list.
- Rate the places and create a review with your comments.

9 TIME TO SPEAK Sell it!

A **Perform the ad that you prepared in class. Record it with your phone. Show your ad to your classmates in the next class. Comment on your classmates' ads. Vote for the best ad in the class.**

10 TIME TO SPEAK Reality TV

A   Go online and search for an article about a reality show that you don't like. In the comments section, make two suggestions for how the show could be better. Think about what the contestants can do and how they can make it better. Explain why these changes will make the show better.

11 TIME TO SPEAK Online videos

A   **Go online.**
- Find a video online that you like.
- Write a comment about what happened in the video and why you liked it.
- Post your comment.

B   **Now find a video that you didn't like.**
- Explain why you didn't like it in two sentences.
- Post your comment.

12 TIME TO SPEAK Places that you'll love

A   **Take a picture of a beautiful outdoor area in your city or region.**
- Write a short description of the place.
- Tell about a great experience you had there.
- Go online to a travel website for tourists.
- Post your photo and your comments.

B   **Wait for friends and people to comment on your post. Answer the comments.**

The authors and publishers acknowledge the following sources of copyright material and are grateful for the permissions granted. While every effort has been made, it has not always been possible to identify the sources of all the material used, or to trace all copyright holders. If any omissions are brought to our notice, we will be happy to include the appropriate acknowledgements on reprinting and in the next update to the digital edition, as applicable.

Photography credits
Key: B = Below, BG = Background, BL = Below Left, BR = Below Right, C = Centre, CL = Centre Left, CR = Centre Right, T = Top, TC = Top Centre, TL = Top Left, TR = Top Right.

All images are sourced from Getty Images.

p. 50 (onion): Westend61; p. 50 (avocado): Richard Coombs/EyeEm; p. 50 (strawberry): ARB/Cultura; p. 50 (lettuce): artphotoclub/iStock/ Getty Images Plus; p. 50 (butter): Chee Siong Teh/EyeEm; p. 50 (chili): fotoARION - Specialist in product and business photography/Moment; p. 50 (cereal): Creative Crop/DigitalVision; p. 50 (steak): anna1311/ iStock/Getty Images Plus; p. 50 (pasta): Giovanni Boscherino/EyeEm; p. 50 (noodles): Pinghung Chen/EyeEm; p. 50 (hamburger): Olga Nayashkova/Hemera/Getty Images Plus; p. 50 (jam): masahiro Makino/ Moment; p. 50 (salt): Kristin Lee; p. 50 (yogurt): clubfoto/iStock/Getty Images Plus; p. 50 (pepper): GregorBister/iStock/Getty Images Plus; p. 50 (corn): photomaru/iStock/Getty Images Plus; p. 51: FatCamera/ iStock/Getty Images Plus; p. 52: maikid/E+; p. 53: Spiderstock/iStock/ Getty Images Plus; p. 54: GeorgeRudy/iStock/Getty Images Plus; p. 55: Jeff Greenberg/Universal Images Group; p. 58: Mlenny/E+; p. 60: chombosan/iStock/Getty Images Plus; p. 61: gazanfer/iStock/Getty Images Plus; p. 63: kzenon/iStock/Getty Images Plus; p. 64 (TR): andresr/ E+; p. 64 (CL): Michael Blann/Iconica; p. 66: Piotr Powietrzynski/ Photolibraryl; p. 67: Fidelis Simanjuntak/Moment; p. 68 (bald, beard & darkhair), p. 83 (icon), p. 90 (boiling, dry, lightning & rainy): bubaone/ DigitalVision Vectors; p. 68 (pierced): bortonia/DigitalVision Vectors; p. 68 (mustache): madebymarco/iStock/Getty Images Plus; p. 68 (hair): AliceLiddelle/iStock/Getty Images Plus; p. 68 (curly): Sudowoodo/iStock/ Getty Images Plus; p. 69: paul mansfield photography/Moment; p. 70: Daniel Limpi/EyeEm; p. 71 (TL): Daniel Diebel; p. 71 (TR): Muralinath/ iStock/Getty Images Plus; p. 71 (C): Babayev/iStock/Getty Images Plus; p. 72: Bloomberg; p. 75: Wavebreakmedia/iStock/Getty Images Plus; p. 76: Anna Pekunova/Moment; p. 77: FatCamera/iStock/Getty Images Plus; p. 78: Jeff Greenberg/Universal Images Group; p. 79 (TL): PM Images/ Iconica; p. 79 (TC): BSIP/Universal Images Group; p. 79 (TR): worac/ iStock/Getty Images Plus; p. 79 (BL): Tetra Images; p. 79 (BR): LEA PATERSON/SCIENCE PHOTO LIBRARY; p. 80: Colin Hawkins/Stone; p. 83 (woman): Granger Wootz/Blend Images; p. 84 (like): pop_jop/ DigitalVision Vectors; p. 84 (friends): Klaus Vedfelt/Taxi; p. 85 (TR): ronstik/iStock/Getty Images Plus; p. 85 (B): Image Source/DigitalVision; p. 87: KLH49/iStock/Getty Images Plus; p. 88: David Aaron Troy/ Taxi; p. 90 (flood): chokkicx/DigitalVision Vectors; p. 90 (hurricane): ayvengo/iStock/Getty Images Plus; p. 90 (stormy, snowstorm & freezing): AVIcons/iStock/Getty Images Plus; p. 90 (windy): MrsWilkins/iStock/ Getty Images Plus; p. 90 (foggy & humid): sabuhinovruzov/iStock/ Getty Images Plus; p. 90 (thunder): JakeOlimb/DigitalVision Vectors; p. 90 (snowy): Color_life/iStock/Getty Images Plus; p. 90 (sunny): StudioBarcelona/iStock/Getty Images Plus; p. 90 (cloudy): Hilch/iStock/ Getty Images Plus; p. 91: john finney photography/Moment; p. 93: Philippe Lissac/GODONG/Corbis Documentary; p. 94: VisitBritain/Gr ant Pritchard; p. 96: JoeLena/DigitalVision Vectors.

Front cover photography by Alija/E+/Getty Images.

Illustration
Martin Sanders (Beehive illustration) p. 95.

Audio
Audio production by CityVox, New York.

Corpus
Development of this publication has made use of the Cambridge English Corpus (CEC). The CEC is a multi-billion word collection of contemporary spoken and written English. It includes British English, American English, and other varieties. It also includes the Cambridge Learner Corpus, the world's biggest collection of learner writing, developed in collaboration with Cambridge Assessment. Cambridge University Press uses the CEC to provide evidence about language use that helps to produce better language teaching materials.

Our *Evolve* authors study the Corpus to see how English is really used, and to identify typical learner mistakes. This information informs the authors' selection of vocabulary, grammar items and Student's Book Corpus features such as the Accuracy Check, Register Check, and Insider English